THE
ROYAL
FAMILY

First published in Great Britain by Colour Library Books Ltd.
© 1983 Illustrations: Keystone Press Agency, London.
© 1983 Text: Colour Library Books, Guildford, Surrey, England.
Display and text filmsetting by Acesetters Ltd., Richmond, Surrey, **England.**
Printed and bound in Barcelona, Spain. by Cayfosa and Eurobinder.
ISBN 0 86283 123 7

THE
ROYAL
FAMILY

The Royal Family

When the barbarian Cerdic waded ashore onto the coast of Dorset in the 490s with a band of savagely armed Saxon warriors at his back, he cannot have had the slightest idea what he was starting. Today, his many-great granddaughter sits on the throne of two kingdoms, which are now united, holds sovereignty over a province and indirect sovereignty over a principality. Furthermore, she is the acknowledged head of a Commonwealth of Nations that numbers about a quarter of the world's population among its citizens.

The members of the British Royal Family are among the best loved, and certainly the most talked about, people in the world. The recent tours undertaken by the Prince and Princess of Wales, and the endless round of appointments for the rest of the family, continually re-emphasise the popularity of the Royal Family as thousands turn out to cheer and wave. It is difficult to think of a time when the Royal Family was as popular as it is today. It does not seem to matter whether the crowds are British, Fijian or American, the genuine warmth and affection of ordinary people for members of Europe's oldest and most distinguished family shines through.

Life has not always been so balmy for the descendants of Cerdic, and over the years they have had to face dangers and difficulties that would daunt even the bravest of men. Cerdic himself had to wrest his tiny kingdom, which probably only covered Dorset, Hampshire and parts of Wiltshire, from the anarchy following the collapse of the Roman Empire. In those savage days, a man's worth was measured by the strength of his sword-arm and the limits of his cunning. In such a time Cerdic made his name feared and respected, and the Royal House of England was proud to claim descent from their mighty ancestor.

Over the centuries the descendants of Cerdic extended their power, first over the West Country, establishing the Kingdom of Wessex, and finally over the whole of England. It was the devastating attacks of the Vikings in the ninth century which produced the most splendid of the early kings – Alfred The Great. In a series of wars, Alfred halted the seemingly unstoppable tide of invasion, and then went on to establish an ordered form of government and justice which serves as the foundation for our present systems.

Other kings of the Anglo-Saxons were less lucky; King Edward the Martyr was stabbed in the back by his stepmother who wanted a younger son to be king; a sorry day for England as the younger son is known to history as Ethelred the Unready.

After the brief, but violent, interruption of the Norman Conquest, the ancient blood of the Royal House of Wessex was brought back to the throne following a cunning political marriage by Henry I, son of the Conqueror. Throughout the Medieval Period the succession remained secure until the bitter internecine Wars of the Roses tore apart the House of Plantagenet and opened the way for the Tudors.

It was this family which threw up the most charismatic of England's sovereign queens, the namesake of our present monarch: Queen Elizabeth I. This redoubtable lady kept in check the violent passions of the Reformation and stoutly defended the shores of England against the Spanish Armada and the wrath of King Phillip. After Queen Elizabeth died childless, the Scottish King James came to the throne of England and united the two kingdoms which had been fighting each other for centuries. During the reign of his son, Charles I, events and personalities led the realm into the Civil War; a war which cost Charles his life and the country its king. It was to be many years before Charles II returned to claim his inheritance and his kingdom, firmly placing the '*noble and ancient blood*' back on the throne.

It was not until 1714, with the accession of George I, that the present branch of the family came to the throne of the United Kingdom. It was this House which brought Britain through her most trying times. The solid, bearded George V ruled throughout the Great War, while his son George VI reigned throughout the Second World War. The blood of generations of sovereigns flows through the veins of the present Royal Family. It is this heritage of the centuries which has made the Royal Family what it is today.

The Royal Family

The oldest, though of course one should never ask a lady's age, and most cherished member of the family is, of course, the Queen Mother. The Queen Mum, as she is often known, entered the Royal Family in 1923 when she married the Duke of York, younger son of the reigning George V. Until that time she was a younger daughter of the Earls of Strathmore and Kinghorne and the darling of the London Season. At the time, the marriage caused quite a stir – it was the first time in living memory that a prince of the blood had married a commoner. However, any fears that the young Elizabeth would not be properly groomed for her role were quickly dispelled during the series of Empire tours the Yorks undertook. During these early tours in the twenties, the future Queen Mother won the hearts of thousands with her radiant smile and boundless energy and humour.

The Yorks were settling in well to the rather quiet family life, interspersed with official engagements, which is the lot of a king's younger son, when the abdication crisis burst upon the nation. After the death of George V, the liaison between the new King Edward VIII and Mrs Simpson became more than a private scandal, it became an affair of State. It was impossible that the King should marry an American divorcee, so he abdicated. This action, hardly surprisingly, caused a serious rift between Edward, now known as the Duke of Windsor, and the rest of the Royal Family. They felt he had failed in his duty, and the Queen Mother was particularly annoyed that he had left the great responsibility of kingship to her less than robust husband.

Throughout the war years, a time of great strain for the new King, George VI, his Queen was a great support and comfort to him and to the nation. Her constant energy and helpfulness cheered the nation, as did her visits to army units and the bombed East End of London. The Royal Princesses were also doing their bit. Princess Elizabeth was old enough to join the Auxiliary Territorial Service Training Corps, where she learnt motor mechanics and encouraged many other girls to do likewise.

During the war, Princess Elizabeth was also engaging in a royal romance which did not exactly meet with her parents' support; they felt she was still too young. However, the young Princess and her suitor, Prince Philip of Greece, had other ideas and won the King and Queen over soon after the war. Consequently, on 20th November, 1947, Princess Elizabeth and Prince Philip, Duke of Edinburgh, were married.

Like her parents before her, Princess Elizabeth did not really have time to settle down to married life before the weight of State responsibility became her lot. In 1952, an obviously sick King George waved goodbye to his daughter as she and her husband left on an Empire tour which took them to East Africa. It was here, at the Treetops Hotel, that the Princess Elizabeth was told that her father had died and that she was Queen. The tour was cut short and the new Queen returned to London to console her mother, who now became Queen Elizabeth the Queen Mother.

Since the death of her husband, the Queen Mother has taken on her new role with enthusiasm. As one commentator once said, 'She has become Granny to the nation'. Her charm and elegance have become legendary and she is inundated with invitations to attend openings and festivals. Despite her age she is always on the go; one of her staff once confided that the Queen Mother seemed to be the youngest person at Clarence House! But this charming old lady does now make some concessions to her age, after all she is now a great grandmother, and spends much of her time at the lonely, windswept Castle of Mey in the wilds of her native homeland.

More than any other person this century, the Queen Mother has played her part in making royalty approachable and human, a far cry from Victoria's view of royalty. There can be no doubt that the cheerful Scottish lass was a great help, after the abdication crisis of 1936, in restoring the Royal Family to favour. And over the intervening decades, as she has increased its popularity beyond belief, it must surely be acknowledged that it is her influence on public opinion, as much as any other, which draws the crowds out to cheer themselves hoarse.

The Coronation of Queen Elizabeth II was a splendid affair. On a summer's day in 1953, the full panoply of state was put on show: Lifeguards in shining breastplates, contingents from across the Empire, 2,000 bandsmen and 10,000 servicemen in all. Tasselled hangings fluttered from windows, glittering lights illuminated the capital and countless parties were held to celebrate the event across the nation. But, above all, it poured with rain. Even so, hundreds of thousands braved the elements to watch the spectacle, while thousands of others viewed the day's proceedings on their newfangled televisions.

The Royal Family

Twenty-five years later, on the occasion of her Silver Jubilee, the scenes would be repeated with even larger crowds thronging round the Victoria Monument chanting 'We want the Queen', eager for a glimpse of the Royal Family on the balcony. Luckily Silver Jubilee Day in 1977 was rather less bleak than Coronation Day had been, and the hordes of visitors were treated to just as magnificent a display of pageantry and spectacle as before. The flag-waving crowds, lining the route ten deep in places, were a living testimony to the popularity of this monarch.

But despite the pageantry and affairs of state, the Royal Family is, above all, a family. The Queen always manages to take time away from her constitutional work to look after her ever increasing family. At the time of the Coronation, Prince Charles was a mere four-year-old and Princess Anne was two years younger. Since that time, Her Majesty has borne two more children and watched her family grow up to have families of their own.

In 1969, a proud Queen Elizabeth invested her eldest son, Prince Charles, as Prince of Wales – the traditional title of the reigning monarch's eldest son. The magnificent ceremony was held at Caernarvon Castle on a dais of Welsh slate. Unlike many earlier holders of this distinguished title, Prince Charles has taken the trouble to learn the Welsh language and to take an interest in peculiarly Welsh affairs, especially rugby!

The Prince has always wanted to get closer to the people he will one day rule and to understand their hopes and fears. It was with this in mind that he went into the Royal Navy. The close confines of life afloat are ideal for learning how to get on with people and how to enforce discipline gently; abilities of great value for the future. By 1975, Prince Charles had risen to command his own ship, the minesweeper HMS Bronington, but affairs of state were soon to call him away from his career in the Senior Service. Among Prince Charles' other interests, polo must rank highly. The Prince is a respected player and can hold his own in any company.

Not all Prince Charles' pursuits are as ordinary as these, and some are downright dangerous. His steeplechasing career earned him a bloody nose when he fell during a race, and he almost broke his neck on one parachute jump when his feet became entangled in the rigging lines.

But the greatest of his adventures – marriage – was not announced until 24th Febuary 1981. Girlfriends, acquaintances and companions had come and gone in the life of Prince Charles, but none had seemed to capture his heart and a few had not met with the approval of the Palace. Being the most eligible bachelor in the world was sometimes a trying business. Every few months a newspaper gossip columnist would write a feature on His Royal Highness' guest at a theatre show and try to read more into it than was really there. Years ago the Prince, in an unguarded moment, mentioned that thirty was a good age to marry. When thirty came and went the papers were full of his earlier comment. But still he did not marry.

It was not until the autumn of 1980 that the papers began to take an interest in the shy, beautiful nineteen-year-old daughter of the Earl of Spencer, who worked in a kindergarten in Pimlico. Somehow the papers had got wind of the fact that this relationship was perhaps more serious than the others. They began to wait outside Lady Diana's flat for the chance of a photograph or a comment, but the girl, though obviously a bit overawed by it all, remained tight-lipped about her relationship with the Prince.

Finally, the waiting and the speculation were over when the engagement was announced and the ring proudly displayed. The wedding date was set for the 29th of July and preparations got under way. Lady Diana attended many functions with Prince Charles during their engagement, at one of which she caused quite a stir. At a charity function held at the Goldsmith's Hall she arrived in a low cut, strapless black evening dress which took everyone aback. At this time, Lady Diana was living with her future husband's grandmother, Queen Elizabeth the Queen Mother, at Clarence House, where she could be kept safe from the prying eyes of newspapermen.

On the wedding day itself the sun shone down brilliantly and London was awash with colour. The crowds thronging the streets of the capital were officially estimated at well over half a million and it seemed as if everyone had a flag, banner or teddy-bear to wave at the happy couple. The bride looked stunning in her ivory silk dress, with its veil and train spangled with mother of pearl and sequins, while Charles was resplendent in glittering uniform. After the ceremony, thousands gathered outside the Palace for a glimpse of the couple and were treated to the then unique spectacle of a royal kiss.

The Royal Family

Since her marriage, the Princess of Wales has amazed the world by her dress sense; designers all across the world watching the Princess for her latest fashions. The high, frilled neckline favoured by Diana swept through the fashion houses of Europe and the lines of her dresses are equally eagerly copied. Almost overnight the world of fashion gained a new queen.

For some years, it had become apparent that Prince Charles was taking some of the official burden from his mother, a process that even led to rumours of an abdication. Since his marriage, this trend has become even more noticeable. Accompanied by his charming and ever-popular wife, Prince Charles is now attending many of the functions and events which would previously have been undertaken by his mother.

The most dramatic and popular of these events have been the tours of Commonwealth countries: Australia, New Zealand and Canada. In these countries Prince Charles, familiar from earlier visits, was welcomed enthusiastically while the cheering for the Princess knew no bounds. It was as if Prince Charles was bringing his bride home to 'meet the folks'.

During the tours, hundreds of small children burst through the railing to meet the 'beautiful new Princess' and she was showered with flowers. Everywhere they went, thousands turned out to cheer and to meet the couple. On many occasions the local police were so overwhelmed by the unexpected numbers that they could barely control the crowds. An added bonus for the Australians was the fact that the Royal Couple had brought young Prince William along with them. This was highly unusual for a Royal Tour and led to many good-humoured jokes and comments throughout the tour, although Charles' remarks about kangaroo meat were misinterpreted. The enormous success of these tours seems to have allayed the fears felt by many at the rise of Republicanism in the Dominions. The popularity of the Royal Family in the furthest reaches of the Commonwealth would appear to have been reinforced.

Prince Charles' younger brother, Prince Andrew, has come more into the public eye recently. His chosen military career as a helicopter pilot in the Fleet Air Arm led him into the Falklands War in 1982. By all accounts he acquitted himself well and, when his ship returned, was given a hero's welcome by the crowds and his mother. Andrew, a strapping six-footer, has always been more of an extrovert than his elder brother, and has a taste for a zany kind of humour. These traits became apparent at Gordonstoun, a favourite school for the Royal Family in Scotland, where Andrew gained his glider pilot's wings at an early age. It would appear that, with Prince Charles married and settling down, Prince Andrew is now taking his brother's place in the gossip columns of the world, while his younger brother, Prince Edward, is only just beginning to step into the full glare of publicity.

Apart from Prince William, Prince Andrew and Prince Edward play uncle to two other children, Zara and Peter Phillips – the children of Princess Anne and Captain Mark Phillips. The Princess and her husband live at their country estate of Gatcombe Park and are well-known at horse trials and events around the country, where they are successful competitors with a string of trophies to their credit. The Princess is also the President of the Save The Children Fund, a cause for which she works very hard.

Today, the Royal Family fills a unique niche in the life of Britain and many other nations. Constitutionally the Queen is little more than a figurehead, though it would be wrong to see her role as merely that of a 'rubber stamp'. It is known that she takes an interest in all of the legislation sent from Parliament for her signature and insists on knowing exactly what is in the document before she gives the Royal Assent. There have also been times in the recent past when the Royal views have been expressed.

But to gain a proper view of the Royal Family in present-day society one must look at its emotive appeal. The Royal Family has become a symbol of what is best about Britain and a focus for all the pageantry and spectacle of the government and the military. For centuries, the rallying cry of Britons has been 'For King and Country'. The two concepts have become almost interchangeable; the monarch *is* the country.

The personalities of the members of the Royal Family, be it the charming grace of the Queen Mother or the dashing adventurousness of Prince Charles, have cemented the place of the 'Royals' in the life and traditions of the nation and have pushed the House of Windsor to new heights of popularity.

Princess Margaret, the Queen's younger sister has always lived somewhat in the shadow of her elder sister and sovereign. However, she has been given her own round of official duties to perform and has attended most of the affairs of state in recent years.

Opposite page: (top right) at Ascot 1982 and in 1981 (top centre), (top left) a film première in 1981, (centre right) inspecting a guard of honour in Germany 1980, (bottom left) at a performance of Swan Lake at the London Coliseum May 1982, (bottom centre) at a garden party at Lancaster House 1978, (bottom right) at the première of Valentino in 1977. This page: (top right) with Lady Diana Spencer and the Queen Mother at the wedding of Nicholas Soames in May 1981, (centre left) at Ascot 1981, (centre) at the Burlington House Fair in March 1982, (centre right) at the ballet in 1982, (bottom left) with the Queen Mother on the occasion of her eightieth birthday, (bottom centre) at Ascot 1982, (bottom right) during the visit of King Birendra of Nepal.

The Prince and Princess of Wales drove in an open car to celebrate the 650th anniversary of King Edward III's charter to St Columb, in Cornwall. While there Prince Charles received a book about British trees, published in 1906 and dedicated to King Edward VII. (Following pages) the Royal Family on the balcony after the Trooping the Colour Ceremony in June 1983.

The 9th of March 1983 found the
Princess of Wales in Devon to
launch an appeal for £400,000
for the county's facilities for the
under-fives by visiting playgroups
in Tavistock and Bovey Tracey.
At the Tavistock playgroup (right
and below) she joined in a
birthday party, singing Happy

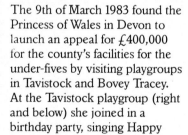

Birthday to three-year-old Emma
Parkin. Later that year, she
visited the Royal Preston
Hospital in Lancashire, the tour,
predictably, included the
children's ward.

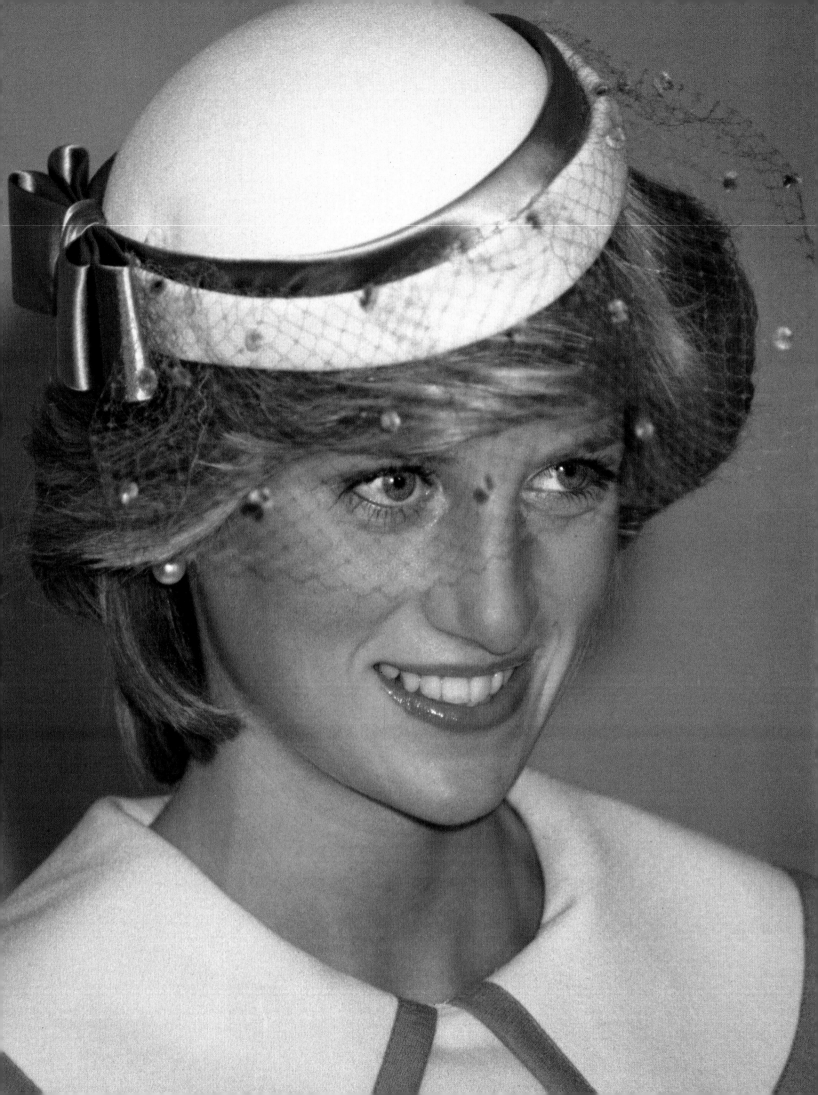

The fantastic reception given to the Princess of Wales during her recent visit to Australasia with her husband seems to have given her added confidence. This was especially obvious at Coberly (this page) and at Canterbury (facing page).

It was a little late for Valentine's Day, but as it was just over two years to the day since her engagement, the Princess of Wales might have thought the heart-shaped bouquet (above) appropriate as she began her visit to Brookfields School for Mentally Handicapped Children at Tilehurst on 25th February. "She's a natural," was the most often repeated compliment. "I'd have her on my staff any day," added the school's headmaster.

On Christmas Day 1982, the Royal Family went to matins in St George's Chapel, Windsor. Prince William, however, was one of four royal infants who were absent. Prince Edward and the Queen Mother could not attend either. Captain Phillips was there (right) with his wife, Princess Anne, and Peter his son. Other royal children present included those of the Kents – Nicholas, Helen and George. Viscount Linley was also there with his sister Sarah.

In recent years Prince Edward, the Queen's youngest child, has been seen more and more often in public. After successfully completing his education at Gordonstoun, where he passed all three 'A' levels and gained an 'S' level, he took up a temporary post as Housemaster at Wanganui, New Zealand. It was here, on April 22nd, that he welcomed his brother and sister-in-law while they were on their tour of Australia and New Zealand. In between times the young prince found time to accompany his family to various occasions.

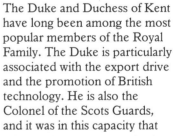

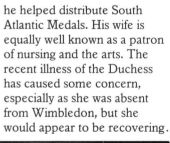

The Duke and Duchess of Kent have long been among the most popular members of the Royal Family. The Duke is particularly associated with the export drive and the promotion of British technology. He is also the Colonel of the Scots Guards, and it was in this capacity that he helped distribute South Atlantic Medals. His wife is equally well known as a patron of nursing and the arts. The recent illness of the Duchess has caused some concern, especially as she was absent from Wimbledon, but she would appear to be recovering.

Princess Alexandra, who is married to the Hon Angus Ogilvy, is the most junior member of the Royal Family to receive a Civil List Payment. She is renowned for guarding the details of her private life from newspapers and the public, while at the same time fulfilling her public engagements with spirit and enthusiasm. However, it is known that she has been blessed with one of the happiest of Royal marriages. Her husband has managed to steer the difficult path between being considered a parasite, by attending all his wife's functions, and being thought of as disinterested, by attending none. The twentieth anniversary of the Ogilvy's marriage was celebrated quietly in April 1983 and their two children, Marina and James are now on the threshold of adulthood.

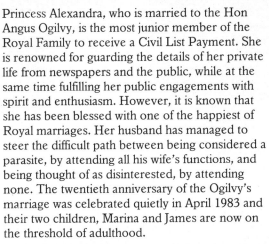

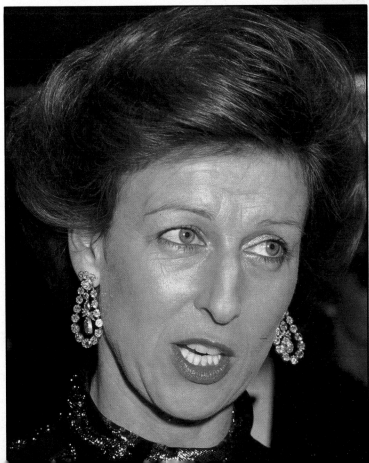

Wherever the Duchess of Kent is and whatever type of occasion she is attending, she always manages to appear in fashionable clothes of good taste, which are also in keeping with the spirit of the event. When she and her husband attend functions of state, (top far left) the Opening of Parliament in 1977, there are few that outshine her. On a more serious note, the Duke and Duchess attended the Family Service of Remembrance at Mousehole for the lifeboatmen killed in the Penlee lifeboat disaster (top far right). The Duchess is also a noted music lover, she is a member of the Bach Choir, and in March 1982 she attended a gala concert by the Royal College of Music Orchestra (bottom).

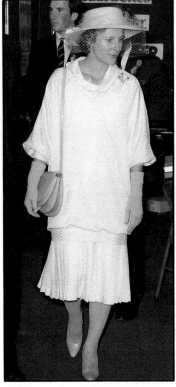

Following the tragic death of the Duke of Gloucester in an aircraft crash, his younger brother, Richard, was raised to the Dukedom. This elevation brought with it a vastly increased work-load. The Duchess, in particular, has been very busy in recent years. Being an accomplished pianist herself, the Duchess is often associated with musical events and organisations.

Prince and Princess Michael of Kent, who have so recently had their marriage recognised by the Pope, do not strictly speaking carry out any official engagements at all. They do not receive money from the Civil List and their activities are not included on the Court Circular. In reality, of course, they carry out some hundred or so engagements a year, most of them to do with sport or the motor industry. The Prince is, in fact, President of the Institute of the Motor Industry and he undertakes over twenty engagements a year in this capacity alone. Indeed, his abiding interest in vintage and veteran cars has prompted him, more than once, to take part in the London-Brighton Run.

"I must retire, with regrets but also with relief, from the many commitments of the past years," wrote Princess Alice, Duchess of Gloucester at the close of her autobiography, published in 1983. For a lady of her age, who has served the Royal cause well for so many years, such a sentiment is not only understandable but long overdue. For many years her staff have marvelled that she could continue to attend so many functions. But her intention to retire was no idle threat and her list of official duties has been dramatically cut to about thirty a year. It is to be hoped that she is as successful in her retirement as she has been in her working life.

Prince Philip has always been interested in sport of all kinds. His abilities as a seaman (facing page top) are, perhaps, not as well known as is his prowess as a driver of a coach and four (this page). He has won numerous trophies at this sport and is a popular and much respected competitor. In 1980, after just seven years at international level, Prince Philip was chosen to captain the British team at the World Championships and he led the team to success. (Facing page bottom) The Crown Prince of Bahrein tries to interest Prince Philip in hawking.

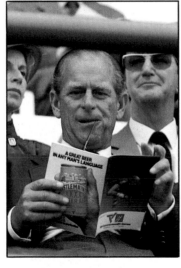

As well as the gala and official engagements which they attend, Prince and Princess Michael of Kent enjoy many sporting events. One of the long term events with which they are involved is the Americas Cup, they gave particular encouragement to the British 1983 entry, *Victory '83.* Wherever they go the Princess manages to look her best.

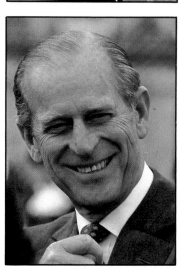

Throughout his thirty-one years as consort to the Queen, Prince Philip has managed to fill the role admirably. His sense of humour, spirit of adventure and ready wit have become popular hallmarks of the Prince as he travels the world (these pages).

It is only a short walk from Windsor Castle to the venue of the Royal Windsor Horse Show, and the inclusion of Prince Philip among the competitors (facing page) was reason enough for the Queen and Princess Anne and her two children Peter and Zara (this page) to be there – at least for the weekend sessions. Prince Philip entered for the Carriage Driving Grand Prix, which he won in 1982. His eldest son, however, prefers polo (overleaf).

The Royal Family, and the Phillipses in particular, are great followers of equestrian events. Both Princess Anne and her husband have been included in the British Olympic Riding Team and they have both won medals. In 1983 Captain Phillips organised a one day horse trials event in the grounds of his country house, Gatcombe Park. After so many years as a competitor it is good to see Captain Phillips taking an active interest in the planning of such events.

heir apparent to the British
one, Prince Charles has been
ged to join the services of
ch he will one day be
mmander-in-Chief. His
er in the Royal Navy came
climax in 1975 when he was
in command of the
esweeper HMS Bronington.
ring November 1976 he and
ship took part in an exercise
e Firth of Forth.
fortunately this promising
er was cut short when his
es as Prince of Wales took
edence. His younger
ther Andrew, however, has
n able to pursue his career
helicopter pilot in the Fleet
Arm, even to the point of
ng part in the Falklands
r.

Prince Charles is now undertaking a much more varied and busier official schedule than ever before, together with many private sporting events. One of the latter which he seems to particularly enjoy is the annual shooting match between the House of Commons and the House of Lords, (above right) in 1980.

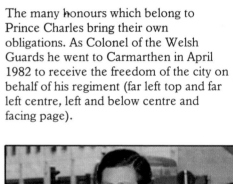

The many honours which belong to Prince Charles bring their own obligations. As Colonel of the Welsh Guards he went to Carmarthen in April 1982 to receive the freedom of the city on behalf of his regiment (far left top and far left centre, left and below centre and facing page).

Prince Andrew's recent adventures, particularly his involvement in the Falklands War, from which he returned in September 1982, and the various rumours concerning his girlfriends, have ensured great publicity and popularity. Though he is determined to continue in the Fleet Air Arm, the new public interest may result in an increased number of engagements.

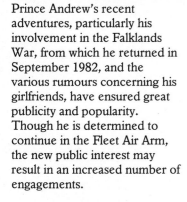

For many years Prince Charles has been a well-known and competent polo player. His Maple Leaf Team, has won several trophies in recent years, many of them due to the Prince's abilities. However his riding skills have not saved him from the occasional tumble on the field. It is on the polo field that Prince Charles is often seen at his most relaxed, thinking nothing of changing shirts in public (facing page top) nor of slipping behind a hedge to answer the call of nature (below).

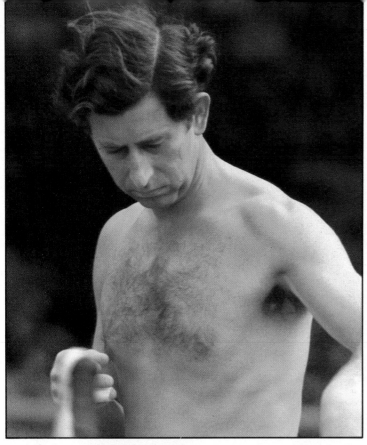

The return of HMS Invincible, together with her most distinguished crew member, was a splendid occasion with bands playing and a fly-past. Prince Andrew admitted feeling 'different' after experiencing war at first hand. "When you are down on the deck, when there are missiles flying around, then at that precise moment you are on your own and that's all there is," he commented.

uring his visit to Rio de Janeiro in 1978, rince Charles threw himself holeheartedly into the spirit of the stivities (facing page). He must have been ore than glad to cool off on the Town all balcony afterwards (this page, centre ft). His first official engagement with Lady iana Spencer, in the spring of 1982, was o less newsworthy, but not for anything e Prince did. When Lady Diana stepped om the Rolls Royce the crowd of two undred was reported to gasp simulta-eously at her dress. The black evening own was strapless and had a daring eckline. Despite the dress, and the athering of notables, Lady Diana seemed oth calm and relaxed on her first official uting as the fiance'e of the Prince of ales.

Princess Anne is not usually thought of as having a direct link with the military, but she is Colonel-in-chief of three regiments. These appointments involve her in many duties, especially visits to her regiments at home and abroad. (Top left) Princess Anne inspecting a guard of honour in 1971, while (above and below right) she attended a passing out parade at Sandhurst in 1973. In 1969 she visited the 14th/20th Kings Hussars in Germany and inspected their modern war machines. She saw the more traditional Hussar uniform when she visited the Kings Troop Royal Horse Artillery in November 1982 (below).

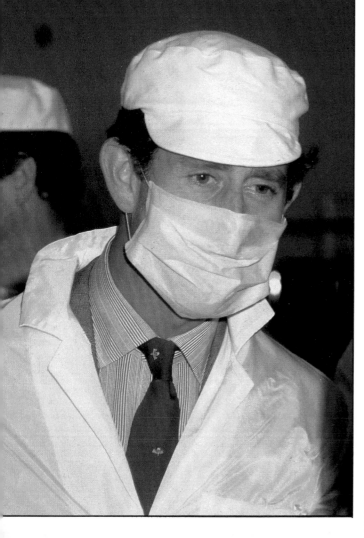

At his many official visits and functions Prince Charles has had to wear a bewildering variety of costumes. Along with the often seen military uniforms, he has worn a garland of flowers on his visit to Mother Teresa's Calcutta Mission (right) and a straw hat to enter the Jama Msjid Mosque in Delhi (above right). Back in Britain, he donned white overalls and a mask to enter the White Room at Brynmawr (far left). This was not for any religious reasons but because the high technology plant demands a dust free atmosphere.

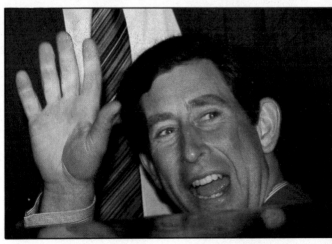

Though the last reigning monarch to lead his troops into battle was George II at Dettingen in 1743, the royal family continues its age-old association with the armed forces, as the pictures on these pages clearly show.